A Country Bairn

Tom Batey

Experiences of Life and Work
on a Family Farm
1933 – 1959

A COUNTRY BAIRN

Dedicated to our Grandchildren

Ewan and Elena

Acknowledgements

This book could not have been written without the help and encouragement of several people. Primarily, Dr. Clive Dalton, a friend and fellow student at Newcastle, originally from Bellingham in the North Tyne now living in New Zealand, for detailed editing and suggestions for topics; Don Clegg for comment and support; my wife Beth, who has been a helpful critic; our late son Jamie for his tenacity and our son Dan for pressing for its completion. The final stage from text to book was undertaken with much help from Stan Owen from the Heritage Centre in Bellingham.

To conclude, I wish to pay tribute to my Father for his resilience and strength of character after being wounded and gassed on The Somme, enduring the loss of my Mother and, with Ma's help, for bringing up 'The Bairn' and encouraging his education.

© Tom Batey June 2020

Front cover: Gilchesters Farm with young Tom and Old Meg

Foreword

By Dr. Clive Dalton

Tom Batey's story may be personal for his grandchildren, but it's also a valuable record of British farming history, of which so much has been lost as those involved never got round to writing their memoirs. Very little changed between the end of the Enclosure Acts in 1801 and the massive changes in farming triggered by WWII in 1939, with the very real prospect of Britain running out of food. A good example is horse traction that only ended during and immediately after the war when tractors arrived.

This farming revolution covers Tom Batey's life, about which seniors will read with nostalgia, and which today's young folk will not be able to imagine. They would argue that you couldn't live without electricity in the house or today's mod cons, no Internet and certainly no mobile phones – and with robots, virtual reality and Artificial Intelligence already in wide use. Then add to this the real concern of the rapidly widening rural-urban gap where children today have to be taken to farms to show that food is not produced in supermarkets.

The story of the farming history covered in Tom Batey's life needs to be told, and Tom tells it magnificently.

If you enjoy this book, you might like to read

Daft Laddies by Clive Dalton and Don Clegg
Just Waffle by Bill Telfer

A PERSONAL ACCOUNT OF LIFE ON A FAMILY FARM

This covers a period from my birth in 1933 until we gave up farming in 1959. During this period, there were profound changes in agriculture from the depression of the 1930s to the introduction of mechanisation and farm subsidies.

PART 1 FARMING AT BROOMHILL 1932 - 1939

Early Days

I was born on 20th March 1933 and was 17 days old when my Mother died of meningitis. What a shock for everyone, although I of course was unaware of this. My only interest as a tiny baby would be food and cuddles. To feed 'The Bairn' Father bought a Guernsey cow, specifically for its rich high-fat milk, not good advice by today's standards.

In my early years, Granny Batey ran the household, a frail and gentle lady in her mid-seventies. Nurse Dunsbury, the District Nurse, who had helped to bring me into the world, was also involved and gradually took over. She had been widowed and had a daughter Cath, 13 years older than me and who lived with her Aunt and Grandmother in Westmoor, a former mining village on the outskirts of Newcastle.

Granny and The Bairn at 3 months

One of my earliest memories is the day my Father, William Smith Batey, and Agnes Dunsbury married in May 1936. Although only three years old, I knew instinctively that this was a special day. It was a weekday and both went off in their Sunday best whilst I was left to be looked after by Granny Batey. I remember them coming back later in the day, changing back into their working clothes and simply getting on with the day's chores.

Ma, as my stepmother was widely known, brooked no nonsense. The house was her domain and, as a toddler, my early steps were restricted to the house, garden and farm buildings. My companions were Spotty, a mature cat, and Old Meg, a collie retired from herding duties. As a small child, I had to fit in with the pattern of household chores and keep out of the way during baking, cooking, washing and cleaning. The only lighting was an Aladdin paraffin lamp in the main living room, the kitchen. There were candles to light you to bed and a storm lantern for use outdoors.

Our nearest neighbours were some 400 metres downslope towards the village of West Woodburn. In one of a group of

Cath and The Bairn

three houses (Parkside) lived the Bells who were good friends. The older members I called Auntie Janie and Uncle Jimmie. Near them was a wooden bungalow occupied by Mrs. Bolam and her daughter Daisy, two years older than me. Occasional family visits were made to Willy and Ivy Bell (no relation to the Parkside Bells) at Townfoot Farm in East Woodburn. They had two daughters, Jane a bit older than me and Kathleen younger. My stepsister Cath would spend part of her summer holidays with us on the farm.

There was very little money around in my early life. Most of my clothes were made by Ma. She wanted to show to friends and relatives that she was making a good job of bringing up 'The Bairn'.

It was a lonely existence for a young child. No playmates. No baby-sitting circles. No pre-school nurseries. No sleep-overs with mates – these social contacts had not been thought of. With no help on the farm, Father was out most of the day, often until dark. So as a pre-school child, you were left very much on your own, to make your own games, inside or out. As a toddler, I could wander through the byres, the barn and the farmyard. In fine weather, I could often be found in the garden, always with Spotty by my side. The garden was large, with pathways between productive vegetable beds and soft fruit bushes. Anything edible I would pick and eat; I had a great love for peas as soon as they became ripe (and gooseberries – picked and eaten raw). However, I survived and, with Ma's experience as District Nurse, I cannot recall being in any way a sickly child.

Broomhill Farm

Although not from the Woodburn area, Father was well known in the farming community. After service in WW1, he returned to farm work and in the 1920s was Manager of a small farm at Medburn, owned by Miss Gledson, whose family were, and are, electrical wholesalers in Newcastle. In May 1932, he married Isabella Murdoch, the teacher at Dalton school, a nearby village, and Miss Gledson helped them to set up as tenants at Broomhill Farm. The idea was that the farm income would be supplemented by whatever my Mother could earn teaching violin and piano privately. According to those who knew her, she was an accomplished musician. Alas, that was not to be. My Mother and Father had less than one year together. It is doubtful if we could have survived financially had not (sadly) Miss Gledson died ca.1938 and left us a legacy.

The house and buildings at Broomhill Farm were isolated and lay just off the A68 not far from the crest of a ridge overlooking Woodburn and the Rede Valley to the north.

It was a purely grazing farm. The land was in two separate blocks, one of grassland around the steading and the other of heather moorland about 1 km away on the Wannie Hills. In the mid-1930s, all farming was in dire straits with livestock being the worst sector. The prices we were being offered for lambs was pitiful, not much more than £1, and wool was sold for 5p./kg.

Because of the tragedy associated with my birth, neighbouring farmers were supportive both socially and professionally. Particularly when Father broke his ankle which was in plaster for 6 weeks (I was too young to remember this incident). When I was born, George Walton of Woodburn Hill gave me a Half-bred ewe lamb. It produced twins every year which were sold separately and the proceeds added to my account at Martin's Bank in Hexham. The ewe lived to a good age and finally succumbed in the big snowstorm of 1947.

The Reedsmouth-Morpeth branch line was the northern boundary of Broomhill Farm. Woodburn station was about 200 metres west from the Farm gate. Every Tuesday, we took the train to Hexham, walking along the track to reach the platform. One day we were late, and I recall being carried by Father, as my little legs couldn't go fast enough. The train was waiting and the Station Master had the tickets in his hand saying "Pay for them when you get back." The whistle blew and we were off. As well as passengers, freight was a significant part of the rail business. Large single blocks of sandstone weighing several tons were brought by steam lorry from Blaxter quarry. These were then uplifted from the lorry by a hand-wound and highly geared chain on a tripod; the lorry moved away, a rail truck moved under on to which the stone was lowered. The highly-prized honey coloured stone was used in many municipal buildings in Newcastle and in Edinburgh – for example the National Library of Scotland and the Scottish and Newcastle Breweries Head Office. When we moved from Broomhill to Gilchesters, someone had the bright idea to use the tripod to load the farm machinery on to the haulier's lorry. So the mower, hay rake, sweep, harrows and household items were brought to the station and lifted on to the platform of the lorry. However, after the shaking and settling during the journey, the machines were locked together. Without a tripod hoist at Gilchesters, there was a great deal of difficulty, with grunting and heaving to dislodge and lift off the machines.

The burning of mature heather was, and is, a well-established

practice to improve its quality for grazing. This was done at a designated time in late winter before birds began nesting. So one day, with sandwiches and a bottle of cold tea to sustain him, Father went off to the heather fell. He lit the heather and started a controlled burn. Alas, the wind direction changed and became stronger. He battled to control the fire by beating the flames with a spade. To no avail. The area of burning heather rapidly grew and crossed the boundary on to the next farm's moor. Meantime, at Broomhill, the afternoon came and Father did not appear to milk the cow. Darkness – and still no Father.

Father and The Bairn at 4 years

I knew nothing of this so it must have been in my first year. Someone went down to the Bells at Parkside to raise the alarm. Someone came up and milked the cow. The village policeman was called who got a group of able bodied folk together who agreed to meet at the Farm if Father had not returned. No sign of him. So about 11 pm, the rescue group set off with storm lanterns in hand. As they were leaving, he staggered in, in a serious state of dehydration. Everyone was relieved. He had battled all day to bring the fire under control with nothing to eat or drink. His tea and sandwiches had been lost in the fire. After drinking copious amounts of water, he collapsed into bed. Moor burning is now strongly regulated.

PART 2   SCHOOLS

Woodburn Primary School 1938-1939

With so little contact with other children, primary school was initially an alarming experience. On the first day, I was taken down in the morning to the school by Ma. And at the end of the day, I had to make my own way home. There were several other children who came up the hill on the A68 to the turn off to Parkside. Thence with Daisy for company along the 300 m road to Parkside until we crossed the railway (no gates!) and parted company for me to walk up through the fields alone. West Woodburn nestles in the Rede valley just over 70 m lower than the farm so it was an easy walk 1.5 km downhill in the morning. No crossing patrols then! But oh, the haul back up at the end of the school day! If we were lucky, the slow moving steam-powered lorry taking massive sandstone blocks to the station would come along – despite shouts of discouragement from the driver, the older boys would clamber on at the back, reach down and pull up the little ones! Then we had to jump off at the lane end.

My first winter was a real trial for a five-year-old. Cracks opened up under the ear-lobes and across the knuckles, developing into painful open sores (termed 'keens'). Clothing was nowhere near the quality of today. I can remember struggling through drifts of snow just deeper than my little wellies, frozen stiff with 'hot aches' to endure as hands warmed up when I got home. Schools never closed because of the weather. Full attendance was required and, if there were more than a few absences, your parents could expect a visit from the 'School Board Man'.

There were three teachers in the school at West Woodburn Primary. I have very fond memories of my first teacher, Mrs. Paterson, whom I went to see many years later. She had small cards with 'sums' to work out and to write your answers on a slate. These presented no problems for me and I was always asking for another card.

Stamfordham Primary School 1939-1944

We left Broomhill at the May Term (the date when all tenancies changed) in 1939 and moved to Gilchesters Farm, a mile out of Stamfordham. This was Father's home area so, although I knew no-one at the school when I started a few days after we arrived, I was known to several children. This made it easier to settle in and find friends. On the first day, I was taken to the school by Ma. She asked if someone would show me the way home at the end of the day. Two boys lived in Hawkwell on the south side of the village and took me as far as their house. They then pointed me to go on to a T- junction and told me to turn right – not knowing that, at the age of six, I was unsure which was left and which was right. I turned left and at the next junction realized that I was lost and so I stood there rubbing my eyes. A lady saw my predicament and asked if she could help – it must have been Mrs. Charlton. At least I had remembered the name of the farm, so she pointed me in the right direction of Gilchesters and all was well – but still a mile to go!

The war began a few months later. The first thing was that we were issued with gas masks which were unpleasant with a rubbery smell and, for some children, frightening. The rule was firm – carry your mask to school every day or you were in big trouble if you forgot it. We had practice sessions to put it on every few weeks and also to march in line into the air-raid shelter, recently constructed. The school was a traditional three-class village school with high windows. Between two of the rooms, there was a row of small hand basins each with a cold tap. No cups – so to satisfy your thirst you drank using your hand as a scoop held under the tap. No soap or towels either; handwashing before eating your home prepared sandwiches was not a priority!

The Primary classes (Years 1 and 2) were taught by Miss Brown, a formidable lady, with no warmth of character. We knuckled down and were taught the basics using a pen with a replaceable nib dipped into an inkwell. Miss Whillance ran the middle classes (Years 3 and 4) a warm hearted and much loved teacher. The big room housed all the senior classes, the 9 to 14 year-olds (the normal leaving age). It was presided over by Mr. Taylor, approaching retirement. His was a very traditional teaching with regular use of the cane across the hand.

In 1940, the village had an influx of about 40 evacuees from one of the Newcastle suburbs. They were allocated to families in and around the village. We were initially sent a brother and sister about my age. When asked the first night what they normally had for supper, 'Pop and chips' was the reply. Poor kids, they were disorientated and unhappy and, not surprisingly, wet the bed. Their clothes and footwear were quite unsuitable for the daily walk to school through wet fields. They were soon re-allocated to another family in the village and we then had Miss Logie, the Headmistress of the town school, to stay – a very happy arrangement. She loved life on the farm and became a close and long lasting friend. The extra numbers were squeezed into the school and teaching continued. About 1942, Mr. Taylor retired and a younger vigorous head, Joe Davidson, was appointed. He began special classes for the 9/10 year-olds in preparation for the infamous 11+ examination which was taken a few weeks before my 11th birthday. I was the only boy to pass, a rare event; the previous boy to pass was Bill Telfer, 5 years before. To mark the occasion, Grandma Stephenson, Ma's mother, gave me £5 – a huge sum in those days. Her weekly pension would be 10 shillings (50p).

Gosforth Grammar School 1944-1951

And so another phase of life began. The options from Stamfordham were to go to Hexham, Morpeth or Gosforth State Grammar Schools. None had boarding houses. Gosforth was 3 miles north of Newcastle on the A1 road. Because Ma had an unmarried sister, Aunt Eleanor, who lived in a small flat, a short bus ride from Gosforth, I went to stay with her. So on my first day, I joined the queue at the bus stop near her house for the No.18, knowing that other children, wearing the compulsory blazer and cap, were also going to the Grammar School. So I got off when they got off and followed them down a street and across a single-track railway line. No gates or patrol. There were few trains as this was a branch leading from a local coal mine.

This was a relatively modern school, being built ca.1930 in redbrick. It was small by today's standards. There were two intake classes, each of about 34 pupils, with equal numbers of boys and girls. The school had an excellent gym with ropes, parallel bars, vaulting horse and ancillary equipment and space for a badminton court, a game that in Sixth Form I played regularly after school. There were two large playing fields with space for football and hockey pitches (no rugby) and a cricket square. I played chess regularly for the school (team Captain and School Champion). I would also play basketball for the school, although there were few matches.

Although I was physically fit and played soccer and cricket, I could not be part of any school teams that played on Saturdays. And I also missed out on youth activities in the

Village that took place on weekday evenings, such as the Young Farmers' Club.

My weeks, and my life and development, were split into two – between School during the week and the Farm at weekends. On a Sunday after lunch, I walked the mile to the village and caught the bus from Stamfordham to Newcastle and then a second bus to Westmoor to Aunt Eleanor's. After school on Friday, I would take the tram to Newcastle then the bus to Stamfordham and walk to the farm. From about Fourth Year, I stayed during the week with Cath and her family in Bells Close, near Lemington on the west side of Newcastle, and took two buses to Gosforth. In Sixth Form, I cycled the 10 km from there to school through the town suburbs most days. One spring morning, I was cycling head-down along Kenton Road through a shower of cold sleet. I looked up to find a double decker bus stationary a yard ahead. Bang! Although badly shaken, I was lucky not to break an arm. The crew were inside having a break at the terminus. They took me in and gave me a cup of tea. The bus was dented and I had to complete a form to absolve them from blame.

Academically, the teaching was good and, after First Year, was streamed into A and B classes. As my school reports show, in the sciences and maths, I maintained a position in the upper quarter of the A class. 1949 was the last year of the old School Certificate which I sat at the end of Fifth Year with good results – enough for Durham Matriculation. This meant that, at 16, I was qualified to enter Durham University. I did not maintain the same standard of academic work in Sixth Form. I was unsettled and unsure, lacking in confidence. This was possibly as a result of being given, for the first time, the information about the death of my Mother. Forms had to be completed that asked for details of 'parents' so the truth had to be revealed. Although none of our friends around Stamfordham had ever sent anyone to University, the Headmaster at Gosforth, Mr. L. T. Taylor, was very encouraging. Initially, I was interested in being a vet and obtained details of Vet Schools at Edinburgh, Glasgow and Liverpool. Unfortunately, my Father's health deteriorated in 1950 with pleurisy and a sequence of heart attacks. Sometimes he was taken to Hospital from the Farm by ambulance, blue lights flashing. Treatment then was bedrest in hospital for a month or more. When he recovered, he was 'signed off' sick and unable to do manual work. To keep the Farm going, my choice of University was then restricted to the nearest, at King's College, Newcastle, then part of Durham University. I applied for, and was accepted, to begin a Degree in Agricultural Chemistry.

PART 3   FAMILY LIFE

My stepmother found that running the house on a family farm was a large contrast from that of District Nurse and Midwife. A nurse was one of the pillars of the community, much respected and well known as she cycled from family to family to deal with any health issues as well as attending to births. On the farm, there were meals to prepare, a small baby to feed and clean, and a house to look after. The work was hard and unrelenting with few aids. No electricity. No 'fridge, freezer, vacuum cleaner, washing machine, food mixer or dish-washer. Non-stick pans had not been invented; only elbow grease to clean out cooking pans. No telephone for emergencies or for social chatting. No heating other than the fire in the kitchen range.

The kitchen was the key room in every farm. It was the only room with a fire on every day, where meals were prepared and eaten, as well as for resting, reading and listening to the news. It was also a nursery for sick lambs, drying clothes on wet days, churning butter, giving one-day-old chicks their first drink and feed on a sheet of newspaper. It was also used to take a bath in front of the fire. The front room was rarely used and the fire lit only for special guests.

In a typical evening, Father would read The Journal and maybe listen to the news; Ma would sit reading a magazine, darning socks, knitting or crocheting. I would read, play patience or play board games with them – Ludo, snakes and ladders or, after the Christmas present in 1943, Monopoly. In summer, I would play outside, make bows from briars and arrows from willow or ash. Occasionally friends from the village would come to play around the fields and buildings.

Church

Both my Father and Ma had a strong religious background, Father as a Presbyterian, Ma as a Methodist. Work on the farm on a Sunday was restricted to the minimum routine tasks. Attendance at Church was never missed. We all dressed in 'our Sunday best', Father in a suit, Ma in a costume or formal dress. As a child, I also had something smarter to wear than school clothes, including shoes. For the rest of the week, I wore leather boots with lots of metal studs on the soles or rubber wellies. We walked to Church for the evening service. This was also a social event when we met with other members from both farms and the village to exchange news and gossip.

For harvest festivals, the front of the Church would be fully decorated with vegetables, flowers, home cooking and a sheaf of corn. On the Saturday evening, there would be a concert, possibly by one of the local village choirs. The Sunday service would be well attended by both members and non-members. On the following Monday evening, everything was sold off by auction to support church funds.

Milk and Butter

To have milk all year round, we kept two cows so that pregnancy and milk production overlapped. The milk was carried to the dairy, cool in summer, cool in winter; the temperature hardly varied. The warm milk was filtered through a cloth sieve, held in a frame. Hairs from the cow and any small bits of muck were retained on the cloth. Any milk required for the house was taken off in jugs. To extract the cream from the remainder depended on the amount of milk collected. Towards the end of the lactation, the quantity was small, perhaps 2 litres or less. In this situation, the milk was left in a shallow bowl for several hours. The cream came to the top and was skimmed off with a sile, a zinc-plated scoop with small holes evenly spaced over it. The milk ran through the holes and the cream was held on the sile to be tipped into a large jar.

In times of plenty, the warm filtered milk was poured into a holding chamber above an Alfa-Laval 'separator'. This, as its name suggests, separates out the cream from the whole milk. To begin, a handle was turned vigorously until the operating speed was reached, signalled by the pinging of a small bell. A tap was then turned to allow the milk to flow from the upper chamber, at a rate controlled by a float, into the heart of the machine. Here, a cone-shaped complex unit spins so that cream comes out of one spout, skimmed milk from the other. The speed of the separator had to be kept up – ping, ping, ping – until all the milk had run through.

After each milking, the milk pail and the cloth sieve were thoroughly cleaned and scalded. Once a day, after the morning milking, all the functioning parts of the separator were taken apart. Inside, there were about 17 cone-shaped interlocking blades. These had to be washed, dried and the whole machine reassembled, ready for the evening milking.

Once there was enough cream, it was churned. If there was a small amount, about 2 litres, a small glass churn was used and held on the knee. With 4-6 litres a larger wooden churn was used which sat on a table. Churning cream was an erratic process and one had no idea how long it would take.

Turning the handle was not hard work but oh so boring. The final precipitation from liquid to solid was quite rapid. But it might be done in 30 mins, more likely about an hour or more. When the slop-slop sound of butter was heard, it was always a relief. The liquid whey was poured out through a plug in the base of the wooden churn, or through a sieve hole in the top of the glass churn. The whey was given to the calves or pigs unless some was required for cooking (it made lovely scones). Next, the butter was washed in the churn. The solid lump of washed butter was lifted out on to a wooden board. Salt was added and the butter thoroughly kneaded with two wooden paddles and moulded into half-pound rectangular blocks. The blocks were then covered with muslin to keep off the flies and kept on a cold slab in the dairy until needed. In the summer months, there was more butter than we could eat. Some would be given away to friends and relatives.

Baking Day

This was usually on a Thursday. Thin sticks would be brought in to give a fierce burn under the oven. After the fire was going well, the flue would be opened and the oven allowed to heat up. No gauges or numbers to follow – just experience. The cloths would be taken off the wooden kitchen table which would then be scrubbed clean. As a toddler, I would hover, but not too close, hoping for odds and ends to eat – bits of raw pastry or cake mix, rhubarb dipped in sugar, apple skins, spoons and bowls to lick. The recipe book (I have it still) would be brought out and consulted. Bread would be made first as this had to be given time to rise. A hot oven was needed so the loaves went in first. Maybe 3 or 4 full sized loaves depending on whether or not guests were expected. Plus a dozen or so bread baps. Then scones – plain, fruit or cheese; some full plate sized open jam tarts with thin strips of pastry laid across; a (real meat) mince pie with pastry top and bottom; a Victoria sponge, and then maybe ginger bread or rock buns. There was plenty of variety. Ginger snaps were one of Ma's specialities (the mixture was always made up the night before) – her recipe:

Flour 1 lb (500 g), sugar 1/2 lb (250 g), golden syrup 1/2 lb (250 g), butter 6 oz (170 g), one egg, I teaspoon baking powder, 1 dessert spoon ground ginger, pinch bicarbonate of soda: warm syrup & butter, mix dry ingredients together then pour in melted butter & egg well beaten; mix all well together. Roll out very thinly, cut into rounds & put on to a greased baking sheet. Bake in a hot oven. Delicious!

Washing Day

Washing was always done on a Monday. The procedures dominated life within the family for the whole day. Just imagine, no electricity, no washing machine, no spin drier, no detergents. The 'Wash House' was a short distance away from the back door, in a row of sheds with a tin roof. Quite a low building, not much above head height. One door, one small window. In the corner, directly opposite the door, was the set pot, a hemispherical boiler set in a brick base with a fire basket underneath. A wooden table, a wringer fixed above a small zinc-plated barrel and a large mangle was the complement of equipment.

In fact, washing day began the day before, on Sunday. The clothes were sorted in the order with which they were to be washed – whites, coloureds, smaller items and the dirtiest last. It was Father's job to bring in coal, kindling and thin sticks (logs) to give a fast and hot burn and then to fill the boiler. This meant carrying water by the bucketful from a large barrel of rainwater nearby. When the pot was full, small pieces of soap were cut up and stirred into the water.

Washing Monday began with Father lighting the fire before seven. After breakfast, the water would be boiling. First the sheets and whites were boiled thoroughly until clean and then lifted out with large tongs into a small enamel bath, a hazardous task, everything still boiling hot. Wound through the ringer, rinsed maybe twice in cold water, then given a blue rinse. Meantime, all collars and cuffs on shirts were scrubbed vigorously on the table before being boiled. After the final pass through the ringer, the damp clothes were hung out to dry on a line stretched between two trees in the close (a small field adjacent to the house). The line was raised well off the ground with a clothes prop. The other groups of clothes were washed in the same way in cooler water. Gales, showers, snow – nothing would put off Washing Day. In wet weather, lines were rigged across the kitchen and the washing hung to dry inside.

Next ironing, also done in the kitchen. The iron was a hollow iron box, the same shield-like shape as those of today. On the flat end was a sliding metal door. To heat it, a solid piece of iron, quite heavy and shaped to fit neatly within the body of the iron, was heated in the fire until glowing red hot. Near the end of this ingot was a small hole. Into the hole was pushed the poker. The hot lump was manoeuvred out of the fire with one hand, the iron held in the other with the sliding door open, the ingot lowered into the body of the iron. Ironing began with materials requiring the highest temperature, then changing as the metal cooled. A second ingot had now been put in the fire, to heat up and exchange in sequence. Health and Safety would be horrified! Then there was the day when the line across the close broke, dropping the drying clothes on to recently dropped cow pats. The family scattered!

Preserving Food

Winters were long and hard. Fresh fruit was scarce, especially during the war. Cabbage and sprouts could be kept over winter outside in the garden, swedes and potatoes were stored in clamps or within buildings. Small quantities of beetroot and carrots were stored in boxes of dry sand.

Hens did not lay many eggs in winter so a crock containing several dozen was prepared in summer using a chemical called water-glass (sodium silicate).

With neither 'fridge nor freezer, a lot of effort was made to preserve summer produce for use later in the year. The garden provided abundant amounts of gooseberries and rhubarb. Some were bottled in sealed Kilner jars, a recent innovation. Much effort was put into making jam. During the war years (and after, while sugar was still rationed), the Ministry of Food recognised the value of jam in the nation's diet and an extra ration of sugar was granted, on request. First, gooseberries, then rhubarb (with ginger). Special expeditions were made (yes, we had petrol coupons to spare!) to collect rasps and blackberries. Wild rasps grew profusely in a former woodland about 4 km away. With the owners' permission, Father and Ma would go off for most of the day and come back with baskets full of fruit. Later in summer, they would go further away to either Hamsterley Colliery (where Aunt Polly lived) or to woods near The Heugh to pick blackberries. The fruit would be prepared, sugar added and the mixture boiled in the jam pan. Meanwhile the jars (very precious items) had been washed and dried. When ready, the jam was poured into the jars while still hot. When cool, they were labelled and put on a shelf in the dairy. One boiling would fill at least 10 jars. At the farm sale, the brass jam pan was sold to Mrs. Wallace for 30/- (£1.50).

Onions, red cabbage and beetroot were boiled and pickled in vinegar. Chutney was made usually with green tomatoes as the main ingredient.

Tit-bits

Although as kids we were well fed at home, there was plenty of scope for extra nibbles around the farm and countryside. In summer, wild strawberries grew on the dykes on each side of the lane leading from Gilchesters to the village. They were sweet and tasty but very small, about the size of a pea, easy to pick but it took a while to have a mouthful. While concentrating on searching the grassy bank, I didn't notice Mrs. Daggart out for a walk from the village. When I responded to her question and showed her the tiny fruits, she took pity and gave me a penny or two to buy sweets, thinking I was so poor. When my folks found out, they were furious!

The bright red hawthorn berries, haws, were edible but there was not a lot of flesh; they were mostly just a hard seed. Hips were also worth nibbling but the small seeds in the centres were tricky to separate. In the war years, the school would organize hip picking expeditions. Several large sacks would be filled to be sent off for processing into rosehip syrup. A few pence per pound would be paid into school funds.

Farms were a great source of tit-bits. Every farm bought in flaked maize with the brand name 'Kositos'. This was a high energy feed for livestock, identical in every way to 'cornflakes' except that it was the natural yellow colour of maize. Regularly eaten in handfuls, it could fill many a hungry lad. There was a mixed feed for sheep that contained several edible items. Groundnut cake (the residue after the oil was extracted under pressure) was very hard but still had a nutty flavour. A real treat would be to pick out from the sheep-feed pieces of locust bean – they looked like dried bananas and were intensely sweet. From summer onwards, there were, of course, swedes aplenty on most farms, perfectly edible when slices were cut off with the ever-present pocket knife. And the garden could always be raided for carrots and, particularly, peas, delicious when fresh from the pod.

Holidays

During school holidays, between the ages of 7-13, I would stay for short spells with Ma's relatives, Aunt Kitty in

Newcastle and the Rochester family in Netherton Colliery. These were quite a welcome contrast from the Farm. The only relaxation for Father was going to the mart, weekly to Hexham on Tuesdays, to Ponteland on Mondays, when selling fatstock, occasionally to Morpeth and, each autumn, to the lamb sales at Bellingham or sometimes further afield to Wooler or St. Boswells. Time to chat and to follow the trade for cattle and sheep, an essential part of farming. And, of course, to buy or sell as required. Ma would also go to meet up with friends, shop or sit in the car to knit.

Throughout my childhood, I never had an overnight holiday with Father. Life on a family farm was very demanding. The first holiday that my parents took together was only possible after I had a licence to drive and could be left with the responsibility to run the farm on my own.

So their first holiday together was in August 1951. After the cow had been milked (earlier than usual, before 7) and the basic jobs done, I drove my parents to Ayr in the Morris 18/6, a large lump of a car with heavy steering and little power. They were booked into a guest house recommended by a farming friend. So off we went before 9, taking over 4 hours via Brampton and Gretna. After Ma and Pop were safely installed and after a short break, I drove back again. The cow was waiting to be milked and was fairly bursting! They stayed for a fortnight and the journey repeated to bring them home.

Meantime, I was keeping the farm going. Twice daily milking and separating the cream, then washing the utensils. Making butter when there was enough cream. A daily check of the sheep and cattle. Make meals. At that time, we regularly took on a post-grad student as a casual helper during the summer months. They travelled daily but had to be given a mid-day dinner. And the summer tasks had to continue, maybe making a bit of pasture hay, fencing repairs and getting ready for corn harvest.

PART 4   FARMING AT GILCHESTERS 1939 - 1959

Gilchesters Farm

We took over the tenancy of Gilchesters, a farm of 104 acres, at the May Term 1939. Livestock, horses, machinery and furniture were moved from Broomhill in a few journeys with the haulier's lorry. I remember the day of the move when, on the A68, the car got a puncture. No spare in those days – a puncture had to be mended. Jack up the car, off with the wheel, out with the tube, find the hole, seal with a patch then reverse the process. Fortunately, an AA patrol was passing and gave a welcome hand.

The Farm was 1.5 km from Stamfordham village, most of the way along a narrow lane (locally called a lonnen) that ended at North Lough House Farm. A gate gave access to Gilchesters land. The house and steading were about 300 m away, on the crest of a slight hill, the highest point of the farm. There was no road – cars and lorries had to choose their route across a grass field. This was not a problem when the land was dry but in winter it required skill and ingenuity to reach the farm.

The house had three bedrooms, no bathroom, a large working kitchen, a small scullery with a shelf and in-set Belfast sink, a front room and an attached dairy. The latter was a low building with a roof of sandstone slabs about 5 cm thick, making it cool in summer. The farm had been in existence since the 1600s or earlier.

In an Antiquity Journal, there was a page showing the bill of sale when the 104 acre farm had been sold from the Cheeseburn Estate. The lower part of the house was built with sandstone blocks and the upper part with brick, indicating a major reconstruction probably about 100 years before. A short distance to the north of the dairy was a row of sheds: a coal house, ash pit, the privy (earth closet), wash house, workshop and henhouse.

Although today's folks look with horror on the idea of using a privy (an earth closet, or netty), they were the only means of performing normal bodily functions on almost every remote farm or cottage. A WC requires a piped water supply whereas most farms obtained water from a spring or well.

The privy was the cleanest room on the property, usually some way from the house and typically attached to an ash pit. The 'smallest room' was about 1.5 metres wide and maybe 2 metres deep, with a concrete or stone floor. The 'seat' was a round hole set in a wooden bench across the back wall and, when not in use, covered with a wooden lid. The bench and floor were thoroughly scrubbed once a week. The walls were lime-washed with white or pink distemper once or twice a year and thus kept free of disease.

The wooden door opened outwards and had a catch on the inside to hold it closed when in use. On the back of the door was a hook, holding a piece of string that held a bunch of pages from Women's Magazines, torn into quarters. No soft toilet paper – but great reading material.

There was no potable water supply in the house, no telephone line nor electricity supply. It was an all-grass farm. There was no barn or granary. Adjacent to the stock byres was a large high shed to store hay with a pitched corrugated iron roof; the rain from this collected in a large cylindrical tank with a pipe leading to a tap in the scullery. There was a purpose-built dipper for sheep on the west of the steading.

The activities described below are typical of tenanted family farms in the area when all family members would be involved in the various and many tasks. From an early age, it was clear that I could never be a livestock farmer as I did not have a 'stockman's eye', the ability to recognise and retain the colours of individual cattle. When I was 'looking the stock' it was a great trial for me if a head count showed that one was missing. I could not recall the colour of the animal that was missing. Fortunately all the cattle had a distinctive 'lug mark'. This was a piece taken out of the ear in a particular position with a special pair of snippers. Each farm had a different position and shape; ours was a small rectangle taken out of the lower part of the right ear.

Help on the Farm

At Broomhill, there was never any paid help although neighbours might turn up at critical times when haymaking, if a storm was approaching. At Gilchesters, there was rather more work than one man could manage, particularly when obliged to grow arable crops. A contractor did most of the land preparation for cropping and was also used for cutting the corn crops. Money was tight so, for a while, we took on a school-leaver, then aged 14. Their wages were controlled and affordable. Hours for paid hands were 0700-1700 with an hour off for dinner at 1200-1300. The problem was that the farm was 1.6 km away from Stamfordham which meant an early start for anyone coming from the village or another farm. These farm lads rarely lasted more than a year.

As soon as I was able, I was also expected to take my share of the work. Physical work became rather less arduous when we acquired the Fergie. I was then aged 13 so took on much of the tractor work – ploughing, mowing and also servicing the tractor. When a retired farmer, George Herron, moved to Stamfordham, we had an effective arrangement that went on for several years. He would work doing any jobs on the farm – but only in fine weather.

When at University, I realized that there was a pool of labour available during the summer vacation. So, for several years, we took on a post-graduate student from June until the start of the autumn term.

Wartime

A few months after arriving at Gilchesters, war was declared. Rationing of almost all foodstuffs was introduced. The weekly amounts for each person were:

Bacon & Ham – 4 oz, 120 g
Other meat – value of 1 s 2 d, (6 p), equivalent to 2 chops
Cheese, butter, tea – 2 oz of each, 60 g
Margarine, cooking fat – 4 oz of each, 120 g
Sugar – 8 oz, 250 g
Milk – 3 pints
Eggs – 1 + an allowance of dried egg
Preserves – 1 lb jar, 250 g, every two months
Sweets – 12 oz, 360 g, every 4 weeks

We had plenty of our own milk, butter, eggs, ham and bacon and rarely bought margarine or lard. I don't know how the local butcher managed it, but we had a joint of beef or lamb most weekends.

After two decades of acute depression, agriculture was now very favoured and required to maximize food production. Although Gilchesters had no barn or granary, we were required to grow crops. A few of the larger and better farmers were co-opted on to the War Agricultural Executive Committee, 'The WarAg'. They visited every farm to decide how much should be ploughed for arable cropping. Their decision was final and incorporated into law. Most of our Front Field flooded every winter and was left in grass. Almost all the rest, some 60 acres, had to be ploughed. We had no tractor, only a pair of draught horses. This area of cropping did not justify buying a full set of arable machinery. The land had not been ploughed for over 20 years so the turf was thick. Two contractors came with Standard Fordson tractors with trailed two-furrow ploughs. These were attached to the tractor with a pin going through a hole in a draw-bar – a simple wooden pin so that, when the plough snagged on a tree root or stone, the pin snapped to release the plough. Outside help was again used to prepare a seedbed and sow the crops – oats, wheat or barley. There were no chemicals to control weeds so thistles were a real nuisance. Harvest was prolonged and hard work. When judged to be ripe enough, a reaper-binder, again using a contractor, was used to cut the crop and bind it into sheaves. They were picked up and stacked in pairs, forming stooks usually with 4 or 5 pairs. These were left to dry for a few weeks, depending on the weather. Next, the sheaves were forked on to a cart and taken to be made into a stack. These were weather-proof and left until winter when the thresher contractor could be booked. Because we had no road between the entry-gate and the steading, the stacks were built in a row close to the point of entry. The first threshing in the winter of 1940/41 was using a steam engine, which was also used to tow the thresher, plus a caravan behind, accommodation for the operator.

Ouston Airfield

As the crow flies, the boundary was about 1 km away from Gilchesters. I remember it being built with land taken from several farms. It was great as a child to go over and watch a variety of planes flying – including Spitfires. About half our Front Field was flat. A number of stout poles were dug in across it to deter gliders from landing! After the war, we were given the poles which were great straining posts for fencing. There was once an air raid and we could hear the Tannoy at the airfield repeating "Take cover, take cover, enemy aircraft overhead." Maybe it was a false alarm as no bombs fell. The saddest memory was when a Spitfire with engine problems was struggling to reach the landing area, but failed, hit trees on the boundary and crashed in flames.

Little did I know that 10 years later I would be a pilot in the University Air Squadron, which moved from its base at Usworth, now the site of the Nissan factory near Sunderland, to Ouston, two years before I left. It was great to fly over familiar countryside and a thrill to swoop a few feet above the heather around Sweethope Lake that was part of our low flying area. Happy days!

Cattle and Sheep

The principal income on the farm was from selling fat cattle and lambs. Although we reared the calf born to the cow, the cattle to be fattened were bought at auction as stores (young animals, 12-15 months old) often in Hexham from Irish cattle dealers. Every animal coming on to, or leaving, the farm, had to be carefully recorded by Government Order in a special book.

Every winter, we had at least 45 animals kept inside to be fed and let out for water every day. They were fed hay, which was enough to sustain them but not fatten them. As soon as there was enough grass in the fields in spring, the cattle were let out and gradually fattened over the summer and autumn. More were bought in spring as the pastures grew. When judged to be fat enough, they were sold at auction, either in Ponteland or Newcastle. During wartime and afterwards, a subsidy was added to the sale price, based on a quality grading system. In a good year, we turned over almost 100 cattle. In 1950, testing for TB in cattle became compulsory and, the first time it was done, we had about 20% reactors which had to be sent for slaughter. Compensation for the full value was paid so there was no loss to us. This test was done annually.

Most cattle that were kept indoors developed ringworm, which was a fungal skin condition. When I got a patch of this on my arm, I thought it a good idea to go into the medical school to let them see it. Such actions were encouraged, as the RVI teaching hospital was on-site. The appropriate Prof. duly gathered a group of students around to show them my ringworm and to snip off a sample. I was informed that I would now be immune from further attacks. I mentioned this to a farmer friend, David Wallace, who said "Rubbish, of course you can have another attack." Next year, I had a larger patch on my thigh. I did not bother going back to the RVI to re-educate them.

In cattle, the lesions disappear when the animals go out on to grass in spring. In humans, the area was covered with a light dressing and a fungicide applied, probably based on mercury. Cattle, apart from the TB test, rarely needed attention. In summer, they might be troubled by warble flies that laid their eggs along their backs. These hatched into fat larvae seen as lumps under the skin that could be squeezed out.

Although some cattle were left outside as 'outliers', most had to be housed for the winter. We kept 40 in three byres, each tethered individually using a loose chain around the neck. One of the most dangerous jobs of the year was tying them up for the first time as most had never been indoors before. First, they were all brought into the midden yard and eighteen selected and reluctantly pushed into the Long Byre. Then the 'fun' began. This was a two-man job (initially just Father plus me as a pre-teenager).

One at a time, they had to be coaxed headfirst into a stall and had to be held there usually with Father at the rear end pushing and twisting the tail. Then, very quietly, I would slide alongside and try to lower the chain around the neck and slip the cross-piece through a ring. If too loose, it would fall off. Meantime, the scared animal would buck and try to kick free. Oh the relief when they were all tied up! Then it was time to go into the house and examine your bruises. Cattle had to be let out for water each day but it was surprising that they soon took to this regime and in a day or two would walk quietly back to their own position in the byre stall – with fresh hay to tempt them.

Sheep, on the other hand, were far more trouble and had many problems. Their feet had to be trimmed regularly, maybe monthly, in wet weather. In summer, they were troubled by blowflies, which laid eggs close to the skin. These hatched into maggots that burrowed into the flesh causing much distress and death, if the attack was bad enough and stock not 'looked' regularly. Infected stock had to be brought in and treated – often with Jeyes fluid after the bare area had been clipped. In autumn, the area around their tail had to be cleaned (dagged) ready for tupping and in spring they had to be clipped and later dipped. Sheep had to be given an oral capsule for worms which had just been developed. Previous to this, worm drenches were fairly primitive. In the old traditional Northumbrian song – 'The Dosin' o' the Hoggs' – immunity to worms was supposedly developed by dosing with diluted pig dung after the pig has been fed large amounts of milk! We kept a flock of about 40 ewes that lambed in late March mostly outside or in part of the hayshed, if the weather was bad.

Clipping to remove the wool was one of my least favoured jobs, backbreaking and hot, using sharp pointed hand shears. Fat lambs were sold from July onwards. In September, store lambs were bought at the autumn sales in Bellingham and fattened. Livestock sales provided a reasonably good income in contrast to the poverty of the 1930s.

Because of Father's ill health, we began to reduce the intensity of stocking. Eventually, only the cow was kept inside during winter. A small number of cattle were kept outside and these 'outliers' had to be fed with hay or straw every day in winter. As grass grew in spring, more cattle were bought. Ewes and lambs were bought at auction in spring and all sold as they got fat. This low input system became known as 'dog and stick' farming.

Pigs

Although there was a row of 10 pigsties at Gilchesters, there was never more than one occupied. Most were used for storage and occasionally keeping hens. It was yet another task to feed the pig twice a day and clean it out once a month. It would be fed on household scraps, any unwanted milk, the whey after butter making and a proprietary meal containing fishmeal. Wartime regulations were that each household could kill only one pig each year. So the pig was huge by the time of pig killing day. This was quite an event although as a child I saw little of it being at school all day.

The process was controlled by the butcher who came early in the morning. The pig was moved through to the garage adjacent to the sties and dispatched with a captive bolt gun. After evisceration, the carcass was hung up and the skin scraped with lots of near-boiling water before being cut up by saw and knife into sides, hams and shoulders. These were rubbed with saltpetre and laid on the dairy floor with layers of salt. Usually another farmer's wife would come to help. It was a busy day. The offal and trimmings were made into sausages (with thyme and sage added), black pudding, grey pudding and potted meat. These were kept in the cool dairy.

The family feasted on these delicacies for a month or so but, without a 'fridge or freezer to prevent their decay, perhaps a third would be given away to friends. This was reciprocal and we would have something tasty when they killed their pig. After three months, the hams, sides and shoulder were taken off the salt bed. The pig's cheek was cooked first and reckoned to be the tastiest part of the animal. The sides were rolled and with the other joints hung in the kitchen until cut as needed into slices or roasting joints. One problem was the proportion of fat. In some of the joints, there would be about 1 cm of lean meat to 4 cm or more of pure fat. This would not be acceptable by the standards of today but, with plenty of mustard, sauce or chutney, the fat was quite tasty.

It was a challenge as a boy to acquire some of the saltpetre. This was much sought after at primary school as a constituent of gunpowder. The other materials were easier to obtain and we knew the formula, not to be revealed here in case this information would have the book banned!

Making Hay

Hay or dried grass is made to feed cattle and sheep during winter when the pastures are bare. It has been a bastion of livestock farming for millennia and is well cited in literature. "Good hay, sweet hay, hath no fellow." (Shakespeare). "There's nothing like eating hay when you're faint," said the King (Lewis Carroll).

The techniques of making hay evolved during my time on the farm. It began with using manual and horsepower only, an intermediate stage when the tractor replaced the horse and the final stage when the pick-up baler was introduced in the mid-1950s.

A field would be allocated for hay and in late spring there would be no further grazing by livestock. The first job was to pick stones so that they would not damage the reaper blades. With an old bucket in hand, the whole field would be systematically covered to collect every stone lying on the surface. When the bucket became heavy, the stones would be tipped out to make a number of heaps to be taken away later. The grass was allowed to grow until judged sufficiently mature to cut for hay. It was a tricky question to balance yield and quality. Good hay would have plenty of leaf and little stem. The next question was the weather and when to begin.

During the war, forecasts by the BBC were banned, so your best bet was to look at an aneroid barometer to select a period of high pressure or when the pressure was rising.

Most farms would use a two-horse finger-mower but we had a smaller version pulled by one horse – the ever-willing Dick. The ribbed steel wheels converted their rotary action through a differential to a reciprocation blade 90 cm long. This cut the grass that moved through a series of fingers close to the ground and an attached board pushed the grass into a single swath about 70 cm wide. There was an uncomfortable metal seat to ride on with the maker's name imprinted on it so a small bag of dry hay was often used as a cushion.

The wet grass would be left for one or two days to dry on the surface before it was rolled over with a hand rake or a turner – a machine with rotating spikes to flick over the swath. This enabled the underside to be exposed to the sun. Depending on the weather, this would be repeated until the whole swath was dry enough for the next stage.

The semi-dry grass was pulled into rows using a horse-drawn rake with semi-circular curved blades some 1.2 m across. The rows of dry grass were then pushed into heaps using a 'sweep' with wooden prongs. The heap of loose hay was built into a cone-shaped 'pike' over 2 m tall with a diameter of about 2 m. The sides were carefully raked to give a surface that would shed rain. Two hemp ropes were used to secure the upper part so that it would not overturn in wind. The 'piked hay' was then secure against wind and rain. To move from the field to the shed at the farm, the pike would be wound manually on to a bogey, a wooden flat trailer that tipped to 45 degrees. This would be backed into the base of the pike and a chain pulled out from a roller and passed around the base of the pike before being wound on to the bogey. The bogey would fall back to the horizontal as soon as the pike passed the fulcrum.

The horse, later the tractor, would take it to the farm where the process would be reversed and the pike slid off on to the ground. The hay would be forked by hand to form a high stack in the shed. The surface would be 'possed' by crawling over the upper surface to make the heap as dense as possible. Children were often called to help with the possing, which was a very hot job when the hay was close to the corrugated tin roof above.

The newly stacked hay often became hot by the exothermic reaction of bacteria consuming some of the sugars in the grass. The key factor was the moisture content of the hay; if too moist, the risk of fire was considerable. Then there was the day when George Herron admitted that he had lost his pipe (a wooden bowl pipe with a silver cover) when forking hay. He couldn't remember if it was lit or not! Father kept watch for much of the night. The pipe was found next winter.

When the Harry Ferguson tractor (the Fergie) replaced the horse, this was a relief for both horse and man. We had a very efficient power-driven mower attached to the tractor to cut the hay. The old horse-drawn hay turner and hay-rake had a draw-bar fitted to replace the shafts and a new sweep and bogey were built by Howard Straughan the local joiner. Otherwise, the construction of a pike and its moving to the hayshed was unchanged – hot and prolonged manual effort.

Working in the hay field in sunny weather was a pleasant job. Often tea would be brought out to the field with scones and cakes. Tea was carried always in metal cans that gave the tea a distinct flavour. While at Gosforth School, the maths Master, George Tully, would come by bus from the town, walk from the village and help with hay making just for the pleasure of working in the sun. He would go back with some butter and eggs. And, later in the year, I would often take a paper bag containing half a dozen eggs and present it to him at the beginning of a maths lesson.

The first time we contracted George Byerly to bale hay, it had already been piked. It was so much easier to bring hay to the shed in bales, each of about 30 kg and, being so much denser than loose hay, the shed was only partly filled. Subsequently, the hay was baled directly in the field after being dried in the swath.

Water

Many farm steadings were located near the site of a spring or well. At Broomhill, there was a trough outside the back door with a constant supply coming from a spring. So all the water for use within the house was carried inside in buckets or basins from the trough.

At Gilchesters, there was neither well nor spring. All the water for drinking and cooking had to be carried in buckets for a distance of 285 yards (260 m). This figure is accurate as it was used to support a Grant application when a tank, pump and piping were installed ca.1950. To fill the buckets, one had to cross a narrow plank (no handrail!) across a small stream on the boundary of the farm, place a bucket under a pipe and hold it until it slowly filled. To stop water slopping out of the buckets on the uphill walk to the house, a light wooden frame was placed across the top of the pair of buckets. This was very effective and stopped the buckets wobbling, preventing spillage. The buckets with their precious load were emptied into crocks and kept in the cool dairy. The water had an unusual property; it was clear when collected but, after a day or so, a rust-coloured sediment appeared. I know now that the water source must have originated some distance away under swampy conditions so that it contained iron in a soluble ferrous form. When exposed to air this oxidized to the ferric form – hence the rust-like deposits. It is doubtful if it would pass today's standards of water quality but it was delicious to drink. With all that iron, it must have been good for the blood!

In the scullery next to the kitchen, there was a tap over a Belfast sink providing rainwater for washing and cleaning but not for drinking. Near the back door, there was a large water butt that was filled from the dairy roof; this was used for filling the set pot in the wash house. Cattle drank substantial amounts of water obtained directly from a small stream that formed the western and northern boundary of the farm. After the water system was installed, there was a trough in the midden yard so that cattle had access to good quality water close to the byre.

A Winter's Day

The routine never varied. The day began just before 7. The alarm would go off. Reaching out in the darkness to stop the clamour, Father would gently move his hand over the bedside table to find the candlestick; then pick up the box of matches in its bowl; take out a match and in the darkness find the striking end and light the candle. He would then get dressed in his working clothes. Walking round the bed, he would light another candle on Ma's side and go off downstairs to the kitchen. First, take off the shade and glass from the Aladdin lamp, light the wick, replace the glass and shade, leaving the light low until the glass warmed up.

Next, rake out the ashes from the grate in the middle of the range and then make paper sticks for the base, add kindling and on top, selected pieces of coal. Using a spill, light the fire, put the kettle (already filled the night before) on the grid over the fire. Now time for a wash of face and hands in the basin on the shelf in the scullery near the back door. In cold weather, the basin would be filled the night before; if it had been a hard frost, there would be a layer of ice to break. There was no bathroom in Gilchesters farmhouse.

Boots on, light the storm lantern and off to give the cattle their morning feed. Hang the lantern on a hook at the junction between the cow byre and the long byre. The cattle begin to stir and get up with a welcoming and comforting snort. They lay in pairs, tethered in a stall with a wooden partition between each pair. In front of them is a shallow trough and a wooden barrier. In the semi-darkness, go back to the hayshed, reach down into a pile of loosened hay using both arms outstretched and grab a full armful of hay, as much as you can hold. Peering over the top, with bits of hay falling down inside your shirt, carry the armful along the passageway and drop it into the trough in front of a pair of cattle. Repeat until all have been fed, 12 in the cow byre, 18 in the long byre. Then take the light on to the calf byre, another 10. Back to the house for a cup of tea.

Time to milk. Collect a clean pail from the dairy. Milking was done sitting on a three-legged stool with a clean bucket held between one's legs. First, the udder was rubbed to encourage the cow to 'drop' her milk. The rub was also to check to see that the udder was (reasonably) clean and did not have any dried muck sticking to it. If it did, this was simply knocked off by hand. No disinfectant washings here!

To extract milk from the teats requires a special strong and muscular hand action beginning with a strong nip between the thumb and first finger followed by a rolling squeeze to get the milk to flow. Both hands are used in a regular sequence on two of the teats, then the process is repeated on the other two. This continues for 20-30 mins or more until all the milk has been lugged out. When in full milk, more than one bucket would be filled at each milking. Fill the cats' bowl (they have been waiting patiently). Take the milk to the dairy. Pour some of the warm milk into jugs for family use. Separate the rest. The skimmed milk is fed to the pig (if we had one), to calves or to the hens.

The rest of the house is now awake and functioning. Time for breakfast – bacon, egg, fried bread, bread, butter and marmalade, never toast; that was a luxury – remember that there was no electricity.

Back in the byre, the cattle have eaten up their hay and are getting restless. And thirsty too. Each beast is loosened and let out into the Front Field to drink their fill at a stream on the edge of the field. The cattle are left out for most of the day.

Then the hard work begins. Mucking out. The muck, a mixture of bedding and fresh faeces, has to be carried out of the byre. Three tools are used, a col, a shovel and a brush.

The col, an elongated hoe, is used first to pull the muck from the stall to the channel and also to pull it into heaps. It is then carried a shovelful at a time and stacked outside in the midden yard. The channel and the area where the cattle lie are brushed clean and some dry bedding spread to give a bit of comfort for the beasts to lie on. This will be a handful or two of uneaten weeds, some hayseeds and maybe a bit of straw. After each byre is mucked out, a feed of hay is put in the front of each stall, ready for when the cattle come back in, later in the day.

Dinner was at 1200 midday, the main meal of the day. A short rest and a look at the paper, The Newcastle Journal, that has been delivered by the postie.

There will also be the sheep to check and feed. They would be counted and 'looked at' to see that all are in good fettle. If we had any outliers (cattle kept outside), they would have to be fed and checked. The pig had to be fed. As darkness returns, or earlier if the weather is bad, the gate is opened and the cattle are let back in. They know there is hay waiting so they each rush to their allocated places to be re-tied. A few other jobs – and soon time to milk the cow again. There was never a break. Farm work has to be done every day – weekdays, weekends, high days and holidays.

The 1947 Storm

The storm affected everyone, not just those in the countryside. Although the first half of January was mild, the memorable storm began on the 23rd. The Met Office recorded that snow fell somewhere in the UK for the next 55 days, until 17th March.

A high pressure weather system had established that lasted for weeks, with a blast of Easterly winds. The month of February was the coldest on record in many areas. The initial snowfall was heavy and regularly topped up. However, it was the wind that caused the problem, blowing the snow into enormous drifts, blocking roads.

The Council snow-clearing equipment was useless – simply wooden V-shaped ploughs that were pulled behind a lorry. No use for drifts up to 3 metres deep or even more.

At Gilchesters, the snow lay 50-60 cm deep across the fields, where there were no drifts. We had a flock of about 40 in-lamb ewes that had taken shelter behind a wall. Our first job was to find them and cut a track to bring them to the steading. Alas, a few had succumbed, including the ewe that had been given to me as a lamb the year I was born.

It was a surprise when Ma heard a voice shouting from the Front Field "Would you like anything from the shop today, Mrs. Batey?" It was Darge Patterson, who had ridden on horseback from his parents' farm 2 km to the SW. He then called at his brother's farm, our neighbours at Thornham Hill.

For about 200 m of the single-track road to the village, there was a tall hedge on either side. This section filled with snow, up to 3 m deep that remained in place for six weeks until it could be dug out manually. Our car was not used for this period.

Muck

For many centuries, muck (from cattle, horses, pigs and hens) was one of the bastions of soil fertility. Indeed, there were clauses in tenancy agreements preventing it from being taken off the farm, as in ours at Gilchesters:

"Clause o) Not to sell or convey or permit to be sold or conveyed from the farm any manures made or produced thereon but to apply the same on the farm ..."

Although the nutrients it contains (mostly Nitrogen and Potassium) can be, and are, replaced by inorganic fertilizers, muck remains a significant source of both nutrients and organic matter on livestock farms. However, in the days of my childhood, before mechanisation, the moving, storage and spreading of muck took a great deal of time and manual effort.

To get some idea of the work involved, a small to medium sized animal would produce a total of about 6 t of manure each year. While inside, bedding has to be added, perhaps 20%. Say, 6 months inside and housed for 3/4 of each day gives a quantity of some 2.7 t per beast per winter. So for our 40 cattle, a total of about 100 tons would have to be moved, by hand effort at least 4 times. First, the daily task to shovel it from byre to the midden. By the end of winter, the heap would be over 2 m deep and cover much of the yard, an area of about 12 x 15 m. Then, in late spring, the now solid material would be forked by hand into a coup (tipping) cart and taken either direct to the field to be dropped in heaps (for later spreading) or to be tipped, forked to form another heap in a corner of a field and kept there until needed. Then forked up again into a cart to be dumped in a field ready for spreading.

One of the most physically demanding jobs of the year was muck spreading – taking muck, a forkful at a time, from the heap and shaking it evenly over the land. The forearms ached and burned with the repeated jolting effort. It was a great relief in the mid-1950s when the first fore-end loaders and chain-driven muck spreaders were invented.

Sheep Dipping

To control ectoparasites and fly strike, sheep had to be dipped twice a year. We were fortunate at Gilchesters as we had a purpose-built dipper that was used not only for our sheep but also by several of our neighbours.

The ceramic dipper bath was about 1.2 m deep, about 2 m long and 90 cm wide. There was a 'well' on one side for the operator to stand in. The entry side had a vertical face. The exit side was gently sloping with narrow steps so that a sheep with its heavy saturated fleece could walk out, with difficulty. The bath was wide enough to allow the largest animal (the tup) to be pushed in and turned over backwards so that the whole animal was completely immersed, including the head. Complete immersion was a statutory requirement with a specific insecticide. The operation might be supervised by the local Constable.

There were holding pens on both sides of the dipper bath to hold about 40 sheep. On one side, catching pens and, on the other, two draining pens with sloping concrete so that the fleece could drain and let the excess dip run back into the bath.

The day began with filling the bath with water and adding a proprietary paste containing strong insecticide. For a while, Organophosphates were used until it was realized these were too toxic for the operator and something less hazardous to human health was developed. As liquid was removed in fleeces, the dip had to be topped up during the day with both water and chemical.

Dipping was a team effort. The key person was the 'operator' who stood in the well wearing an old hat, a pair of goggles, a worn out rubberised Mackintosh, not much else underneath and a pair of wellies. I did the job for 10 years and it was hot and disagreeable. The 'catcher' would grab hold of a sheep by its fleece, push it to the edge of the dipper and drop its back legs down into the fluid. The operator would take the sheep by the neck and pull it over backwards to make sure that the head was fully under the liquid for about half a minute, as required by law. Of course, the sheep struggled and spluttered. It was then helped to roll over into an upright position and on to its feet so that it could stagger up the steps out of the dipper into the draining pen. The drenched sheep would drain until all drips had stopped and then be moved out. The operator was, of course, drenched in the smelly toxic liquid. Fingernails would be yellow stained for some weeks afterwards. There were several instances of operators showing clear signs of Organophosphate poisoning until these chemicals were banned. Before the dip was emptied, it was common practice to plunge the collie dog into the dip!

At the end of the day, a plug would be removed at the base of the bath and the liquid released. It ran through a pipe and out on to the edge of a field and allowed to soak into the ground, well away from a stream.

Cars

On an isolated farm, a car is very much part of life. Not a luxury, a necessity. During the war, petrol was rationed and travel was restricted to business use only – but of course we used the car to visit friends.

As far as the first car that I can remember, the least said the better. An Austin 7 in poor condition that was eventually exchanged in 1938 for a second-hand Ford 8, costing £80. It ran well and was a sturdy workhorse and work it did. It was also unique in the economic sense as it was sold for twice what we paid for it after 10 years' use. The only snag was that it was a bad starter. A pull on the electric starter would work but only when the engine was warm and occasionally in summer. Cars of that era had a starting handle. This was inserted through a hole in the front bumper. Turning the handle was a jerky rotating motion as the pistons went through the cycle of compression – and hopefully ignition. Using the handle required skill. The thumb had always to be placed around the handle alongside the fingers. If the engine decided to partially ignite on the wrong part of the combustion cycle, a not infrequent occurrence, a kick back through the handle would give a fierce and sudden jerk to the hands. If the thumb was wrapped around the handle, a dislocation was likely. So hand starting was not a job for the inexperienced, however strong and enthusiastic.

Starting in winter was an absolute nightmare. So Father decided to harness alternative horsepower, literally, Dick, the horse. Although not a heavyweight, he was a bright and willing friend. So the car was pushed out of the garage manually to face down the farmyard. The windscreen was wound open. This is a feature which seems unusual today, but was then normal on all cars. A light harness was placed on Dick's back, and the reins fastened to the bridle. The horse was then backed up a short distance in front of the car, a chain from the harness was attached to each end of the front bumper and the reins passed through the open windscreen. The whole operation was a solo effort designed by Father. "Gee up" was the call. The horse walked forward pulling the car with Father holding the reins and the steering wheel at the same time, no mean feat. The car was slipped into gear, the clutch released and the walking horse turned over the engine. When the engine fired and was running, "Whoa" brought the horse to a stop. In fact, it didn't take long for dear old Dick to learn that as soon as the engine started, he had to stop. No call was needed.

On a farm, a car was not just for carrying passengers. A calf bought at market would have its legs and lower body tied into a sack, which was put on the back seat. The smell of a calf was reasonably acceptable. Sheep were something else. When times were hard, the slab of the back seat was taken out and 4 or even 5 sheep put in. The more, the better in one sense. If they were tightly packed, they couldn't jump into the front. But the smell emanating from hot sweaty sheep, panting away over your shoulder and down the back of your neck, was something to turn the stomach. And then, one day, a sheep put its head through the back window. At least it let in some air.

Headlights were so poor that in foggy weather, or when the windscreen was frosted over, the windscreen was opened to peer through. Sprays for de-icing were not available. Heaters did not exist. So travel in winter could be a bitterly cold experience, even when wrapped up with gloves, scarves and rugs.

Safety features were almost non-existent. There were no side mirrors, only a small mirror in the centre of the front windscreen. This gave a restricted view, looking back through a small rear window. Indicators did not flash, they consisted of a short horizontal arm in the side of the car worked by a solenoid, which, when the switch was activated, flicked the arm upwards into a horizontal position, sticking out from the side of the car for about 15 cm. Inside the arm was a small bulb, giving out a barely-visible orange glow. Of course, most signals were made by hand through the open window – a compulsory part of the driving test.

The custom for farmers' sons was that they learned to drive as soon as their legs were long enough to reach the pedals. I was 13 when Cath's husband taught me the rudiments by driving across farm fields. The driving test was booked for a few months after your seventeenth birthday. During that period, three lessons were taken with one of the town driving schools. This was to have the experience of driving in dense traffic in the vicinity of the Test Examiner's Office. A pass was expected as we had been driving then for four years, and often on public roads.

The Little Grey Fergie

Harry Ferguson, an Irish-born British mechanic, was a genius. Before his inventions were introduced, a tractor was simply a means of providing traction, to pull or push a piece of machinery. The Ferguson tractor had a three-point linkage with hydraulics, which meant that a plough or other attachments were integrated into one unit.

We bought one of the early Fergusons in 1946 together with a transport box, a two-furrow plough, a tined cultivator and a fully-mounted mower. Our other machinery was converted for tractor use with a drawbar to replace the shafts. The Fergie ran on petrol that was still rationed. The petrol was sold without tax and dyed red so that it would be easily detected, if used illegally in private cars.

The mower was driven from the power shaft so had no wheels. It could cut a dense crop without difficulty. I was sometimes contracted to cut a neighbour's hay, if it was wet and heavy. Corners were also cut easily as the cutter-bar could be raised hydraulically and the tractor reversed – a manoeuvre not possible with a trailed machine.

The technique of reversing a trailer is not instinctive and takes a while to learn. When school friends were visiting and keen to 'have a go' on the tractor, I would tease them by driving it, with a trailer attached, a short way into a field and ask them to reverse it through a gate. I would go off into the house and come back 20 minutes later to find them still struggling and often further away from the gate.

45

The Saw Bench

When the Royal Agricultural Show came to Newcastle in 1956, I had a pass for the week. My supervisor, Fred Hunter, had set up a display about the Chillingham Wild Cattle Association, as he was its Secretary. This achieved a degree of notoriety in the press as the smallest breed in Britain. As helpers, we were required to project, on request, a sequence of slides on a screen in a small tent. It gave me plenty of time to look through the machinery displays. I was intrigued by a saw bench, mounted on the three-point linkage of a Ferguson tractor. I persuaded Father to buy it – the one on display. My idea was that this might be of better quality than one off the standard production line. So when the Show ended, the next day I drove the Fergie the 14 miles to the Showground to collect it.

Circular saw benches are notoriously dangerous. Most are simply a strong metal table with a slot in the centre for the blade. Wood to be cut would be slid across the table to engage with the fast-spinning blade. The Howard saw bench was hinged so that the log to be sawn was lifted on to the bench and, resting on a cross-piece, was gently pushed towards the blade for cutting. The blade of 75 cm diameter was driven off the power take-off, which whistled when at full speed. When the slice was separated, the table moved back, the cut slice thrown to one side, the log moved across and the cut repeated. I always wore heavy leather gloves as one's hands were only a few centimetres from the spinning blade.

In almost every farmyard there was a large pile of wood, a collection of fallen trees and old fence posts. There was a good opportunity for me to make a bit of money. So on many Saturdays in winter, I went off around the area cutting logs for, I think, £3 per hour: sheer profit for me as Father paid for the fuel. After a few days' work, the saw blade had to be sharpened and set. Although it was a rather crude method,

I found it possible to set the individual teeth by eye using an adjustable spanner to grip and widen the gap.

Country Travellers

In the late 1930s, just before the war, isolated farms had a succession of callers. Travellers were not the caravan dwellers we know today but were what would now be called 'trade representatives'. At this time, farming was at a low ebb. Few farms had telephones. Not all had a car. So the traveller was a welcome visitor and would be sure of a cup of tea with scones and cake on offer or maybe even a hot meal.

Tom Straughan came to Broomhill Farm once a month from his shop in Stamfordham to take his order for groceries. He had known my Father since schooldays; he was a good businessman and had an extensive country round. Over his tea, he would write carefully in a duplicate order-book all that was required – flour, sugar, tinned goods, biscuits, fruit, sweets (NO butter or tea). And usually with a suggestion for something extra, maybe a box of chocolates (a good salesman!). He would also go off with a cheque to settle the previous month's order. Two weeks later, a small lorry would arrive with a young man delivering a box containing everything ordered. Surprisingly, this was like the current trend for on-line ordering. Alas, all this came to an end in 1939 when the lorry driver was called up and petrol was rationed.

Although I do not remember, at some time in the mid-1930s, we had a visit from a salesman of a tea wholesaler in Edinburgh, Matheson McLaren & Co. So every quarter, a box came through the post containing eight x one-pound packets of loose tea (no tea bags in those days). Then, when the war came, tea was rationed. The same boxes of tea came regularly each quarter. Our tea coupons were sent to Edinburgh with a cheque for payment. This quantity was comfortably enough for our needs and town relatives were often given some to take home. After the end of the war and whilst it was still rationed, we had a visit from the (new) salesman from the Wholesaler. He was aghast – we had been receiving at least one third more than our ration! So, for a year or two, we had to suffer like everyone else with only 60 g a week each.

The salesman from Otterburn Mill, which was still operating then, called maybe once a year. He knew where he would get a decent cup of tea and a light meal. He was very confident "The rugs sell themselves," and would often make a sale. The quality of the wool rugs was legendary. We still have one.

Waste Not

In the old days, nothing left the farm, except farm produce – grain, livestock, wool, eggs and butter. No council bin collection (no bins), no bottle banks or recycling centres. Paper had many uses. Used newspapers were used to light the fire. Some were twisted into lighting spills for smokers and to light candles. The village stores sold out-of-date newspapers in bundles. The pages of women's magazines were cut into squares, threaded on a string and placed behind the door of the outside privy. Paper bags for sugar and flour were either reused or burnt. Lemonade and Tizer bottles were returnable. Other glass bottles, such as those containing fruit squash, were kept; they had many uses – for feeding pet lambs, or dosing cattle with medicines. Tin cans might be flattened and nailed over rat holes in the buildings. Otherwise, cans and unwanted small bottles, such as those containing meat paste, would be thrown in a corner of the stack yard and would soon be lost to sight in a patch of nettles. Every farm had an area of rough ground, or an out of the way corner, where odds and ends were dumped. These could be a great source for future archaeologists, although not environmentally friendly. Sacks used to deliver flaked maize and other feed were kept, as they were made of hessian and reused to carry feed to sheep, to wrap up a sickly lamb or even as a shoulder cape in wet weather. Or they might be used as the base for a proggy rug.

The trimmings of vegetables and fruit from food preparation were simply thrown into the stackyard for the hens to fight over or were given to the pigs, which also received the separated milk and whey. There was no interest in, or need for, composting!

The stone built ash pit had an open front into which was thrown the daily output from the fire. It was, by design, adjacent to the privy. The lower part of the wall of the latter had an opening into the ash pit. It was an annual chore to shovel out the contents of both privy and ash pit into a cart, then to be spread on the land. Waste collection by the Council did not begin until several years after the war when they used a small specialized truck to pull alongside the ash pit enabling the ash and ordure to be thrown in and taken to landfill. Not a popular job!

It is a normal and sad fact of farming that animals die unexpectedly. Sheep and lambs would be taken to an area of soft ground to be buried in a hole dug by hand. Cattle, however, were taken away by a specialist company of knackers. They would be called by telephone and, within a day, a small lorry would arrive.

This had a back door that lowered to the ground, leaving a sloping ramp. A chain was pulled out, long enough to reach the rear legs of the dead beast, even if it was inside a byre. The chain would be wound in on a geared roller with a handle turned manually and the animal dragged on board. The carcass was destined for the knacker's yard in Gateshead for dismemberment and rendering into fertilizer. About a year later, the farm would receive a cheque for at least £1.

The Farm Garden

The Broomhill garden no doubt had rows of different vegetables but the only crop that I remember was peas. As soon as they were ripe, I loved their sweet taste and soon learned how to break open the pods to reveal their contents. Deep purple irises grew near the front door and these remain one of my favourite flowers.

At Gilchesters, there were two gardens, one in front of the house with flower beds and vegetables, and there was another across the close for vegetables only. One thing every farm garden was never short of was fertility in the form of a load of well-rotted muck. A cart load would be dropped at the gate and forked into the garden on a wheelbarrow. The patch of rhubarb got a thick layer every year so the flowering stem grew to a height of 2 metres and, if unpicked, the stems could be thicker than your arm and leaves like an umbrella. In spring, a few old buckets were upturned over the roots to force some early pink tender stems.

One of the spring rituals was a trip to collect pea sticks, which were off-cuts from small pine or spruce branches. The ends were pushed firmly into the ground to form a double row to support the peas as they grew and climbed. We gathered them in a wood near Cheeseburn Grange with the forester's permission. He was an old friend of Father's. Potatoes of an early variety would have a layer of muck put along each open trench and the sets planted directly on it. Cabbage lettuce would produce heads about 50 cm cross, if seedlings were thinned out. Radish reached the size of walnuts. There were three gooseberry 'shrubs' that were so large you could hardly call them bushes.

Leeks, Brussels sprouts, cauliflowers and cabbage were bought at the Market as plants. Garden seeds were bought in Hexham at a specialist shop, called William Fell. As grass seeds for the farm were bought in large quantities, seeds for the garden were provided free. Long after Father retired and moved to Wylam, every spring he would go into Fell's seed shop and pick up the packets he needed – lettuce, radish, beetroot, carrots, peas, beans. Father made sure that the farm salesman was there so that he was able to go past the till with a smile and a comment from the salesman – "Of course Willy can have the seeds – he was a good customer when on the Farm."

Young Farmers' Club

The YFC's were, and are, an important part of country life. They gave regular social contact, education in a wide range of topics and competitions at local and national level. While at school, I was unable to take part, as meetings of our local Club were held in Stamfordham on a Monday evening. Once at University, however, I was a regular member, eventually joining the Committee and becoming Chairman.

Visits to farms and local industries were a popular part of the programme, as were stock judging competitions. One annual event gave rise to real fear and apprehension – public speaking competitions. These took place in one of the local halls with an audience of members from the other clubs in South Northumberland together with many parents. There were several classes but the one most feared was the unprepared talk. You had to select one of three slips of paper held out by the organiser. This gave you a topic on which you had 20 minutes to prepare and then present a 10 minute talk. Not nine minutes, not eleven but exactly 10. You had no idea what topics might come up. Such experience gave one confidence to respond if unexpectedly being asked to comment at a meeting or conference. I have always felt gratitude to the YFC movement for this experience and of other activities that were an important part of character development.

The Farm Sale

This took place on 26th September 1959, the year my Father became 65 and a few days before I left to pursue a career as a soil scientist. The preparation for the sale took most of the summer with help from farming friends, particularly the Patersons and Wallaces.

There were two aspects to leaving the farm, tenant rights and the livestock, machinery, etc., that had to be disposed of. Tenant rights included the value of buildings and other fixtures that we had taken over on entry – the large hayshed, the bull pen and the sheep dipper, plus any improvements that we had made – the diesel tank, the farm road and the installation of electricity.

These had to be professionally valued and a formal agreement drawn up. One agent was appointed on behalf of the tenant, the other representing the landlord. The valuers also had to walk the farm to assess the quality of the grass and crops, the fencing, the rotation and the residual value of any lime and fertiliser applied in the last few years. Anything not up to standard would be deducted as 'dilapidations'.

The second was selling all the livestock and 'deadstock'. Auctioneers were appointed (Iveson and Walton) who advertised the sale in the press. A simple sale ring and holding pens were constructed for the livestock. A total of 44 sheep were sold for an average of £5.95 and 40 cattle, with the mature cattle averaging £54, with a top of £65.

The tractor, machinery and other materials were cleaned and laid out in rows across the Front Field. Furniture and many household items were also sold, if not wanted in the newly-bought house in Wylam. To pay for the services of the auctioneer, every buyer had to pay a commission of 10% added to the purchase price.

Post-Farming

On retirement in 1959, my parents moved to Wylam. My Father enjoyed gardening and went weekly to the mart at Hexham to meet up with farming friends. Health-wise, he continued to have heart attacks from which he recovered at home by simply having a few days in bed. He had a stroke in August 1979 and died in Hexham Memorial Hospital, with a school friend, Jack Straughan, ill in the next bed.

Although brought up in the relative poverty of the pre-war years, the author was encouraged by his family to take full advantage of the benefits of the 1944 Education Act, through school and University. In his first year at the Grammar School, fees were paid for which he took a cheque for £10 each term. His career as a soil scientist took him to many countries but always close to those who gain a living from the land.

Farewell to Gilchesters Farm